HUNGOVER
OWLS

HUNGOVER
OWLS

J. PATRICK BROWN

ABRAMS IMAGE, NEW YORK

Editor: Wesley Royce
Designer: Laura Crescenti
Production Manager: Anet Sirna-Bruder

Library of Congress Cataloging-in-Publication Data:

Brown, J. Patrick.
 Hungover owls / J. Patrick Brown.
    p. cm.
 ISBN 978-1-4197-0083-5
 1. Alcohol—Physiological effect—Humor. 2. Owls—Humor. 3. Wit and
humor, Pictorial. I. Title.
PN6231.A448B76 2011
818'.602—dc22

                    2011008540

Abrams Image books are available at special discounts when
purchased in quantity for premiums and promotions as well as
fundraising or educational use. Special editions can also be created
to specification. For details, contact specialsales@abramsbooks.com
or the address below.

THE ART OF BOOKS SINCE 1949
115 West 18th Street
New York, NY 10011
www.abramsbooks.com

AUTHOR'S NOTE

IT STARTED, APPROPRIATELY ENOUGH, THE MORNING AFTER.

I awoke from a rather ill-advised red wine binge to the kind of "sinus infection" that you get after putting away a good half gallon of crimson regret. There was something the size of a grapefruit lodged fairly firmly in the front part of my brain, and having blinked, like, at least six times, I was all good for my physical activity of the day.

"Auspicious" wasn't exactly the word for it. "Oh God, why?" would have been a closer assessment of my thoughts, if not an exact quote.

Unfortunately, one of my asshole friends had to go and pull the major dick move of being born on this inconvenient date, so rather than getting to spend the morning catching up on my groaning and counting the rotations of my ceiling fan, I had to go and drag myself over to her apartment to drop off her present— as well as a couple of choice excuses.

Oh no, I can't stay. Yeah, really bad allergies. Yeah, see the ruddy complexion? That's, uh, that's allergies. Yeah, the teeth too. All part of that same system. Fuckin' hay fever, am I right?

In an effort to at least *pretend* that I wasn't blowing off her party to go cuddle up with a trash can, I let my friend show me some of the gifts she had received from her significantly better friends. One of them was a copy of *The Tale of Squirrel Nutkin* by Beatrix Potter. I opened it up, and there was an illustration of Old Brown, an otherwise benevolent owl driven to murderous rage by the constant onslaught of the mischievous Nutkin's bullshit.

Man, that owl and I understood each other.

"This owl is hungover," I said. "Now that I think of it, I'm pretty sure that all owls are hungover. It is important that I leave immediately so that I may gather evidence to prove this."

And that was that. It was all terribly neat and reasonable.

A few hours later, after the last of my spasms had ceased and I was certain that the thing that had come out of me wasn't vital to my continued survival, I decided I would actually do the thing that I had said I'd do. A novel concept, and one that I'm still getting the hang of.

So I put together a pretty compelling argument, and sure enough, people agreed with me. A lot more people than I had expected. Hell, a lot more people than I ever would have imagined pretty much period.

"Overwhelmed" would be the exact word for it. Or maybe even "Oh God, why?"

As I got more and more responses, I grew more and more incredulous. Disbelief led to whiskey, whiskey led to agony, and agony led to material.

There's just no way I can stress enough how much *fun* these past few months have been, and I want you to share in the slack-jawed, giddy awe that has loomed over the whole thing.

So, thank you. Yes, you. You helped to convert a lifetime's worth of guilt into childish glee and taught me more about those feathered bastards than I would have ever dreamed. Because honestly, what sort of dork dreams about owls?

Well, I mean, I do *now*, but . . . well, there you go.

Anyhoot. Have one on me and the rest of the high-crested crew, and don't you dare fly yourself home.

—**J. Patrick Brown**

"OH,
AREN'T YOU
SPECIAL,
WITH ALL YOUR . . .
STANDING . . .
AND
SHIT."

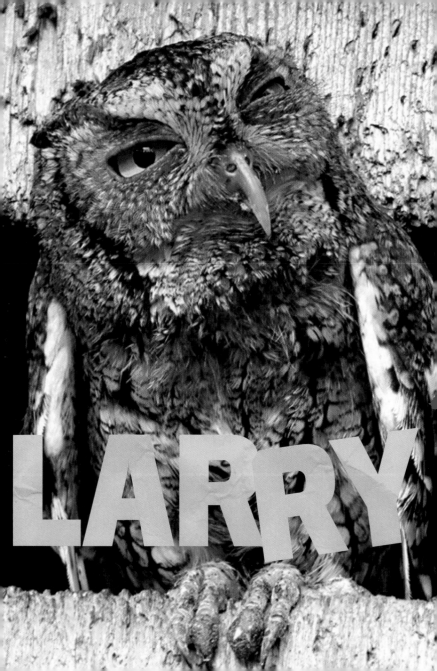

WEARING A DRESS WASN'T *ENTIRELY* OUT OF LARRY'S REALM OF EXPERIENCE, SO HE WAS ADMITTEDLY LESS SURPRISED THAN HE PRETENDED TO BE.

"I am wearing a dress," Larry said aloud, noting that his vocal chords had grown raspy and rusted from what felt like centuries of disuse. "I also appear to be on a mattress," he added, with no small swell of pride. While he was more or less sure that the circumstances that had led him to be bedecked in puke-streaked polka dots would ultimately reflect upon him poorly at the end of the day, at least he knew what he was supposed to sleep on.

"So there," Larry said, to nobody in particular.

Larry frowned, causing a rustle of fabric by his chest. He hadn't meant to move anything other than his face. Apparently, at some point last evening, the entirety of his muscles had been fused into one large clump. Here he was, on the business end of various Sorrowful Mysteries: What had he done? Where was he? Who was the owner of this knee-length number? And why was he wearing it? And for the aching half-life of him, Larry couldn't give what shits he had left. If he had managed to boot last night, then he had booted what remained of his curiosity.

Larry lay there, enumerating his miseries and taking a profound delight in opting out of their profundity. So he was in a dress, somewhere strange, roughly three-quarters quadriplegic. *Pshaw*. For all he cared, he could have woken up on a roller coaster wearing a blood-stained mascot's outfit and clutching a bucket of body parts. Which would go a long way toward explaining that smell, not to mention the fact that his stomach appeared to be experiencing centrifugal force.

Guilt taunted Larry from the edges of his literal unconscious, and yet he would not be moved. At least not for another five minutes. His six-by-eight stained domain wasn't much, but for as long as Larry lay there, it was his. This was his last stand, his Fortress of Solitude, his Point Lookout. Reality and its scavengers stood poised to tear him down to component shame, but so long as Larry maintained his death grip on the world of the horizontal, nothing could touch him.

Larry leaned back a little more than he had intended to and closed his eyes. There would come answers in time, sure. But for this last, best moment, they could fuck right off to that slushy no place from whence they came.

Then, before he could react, which isn't really saying very much, there was a driven, intentioned clicking of a door. A step was all it took for Larry, face full of last night's heat, to feel the incredulous gaze of encroaching unpleasantness.

"Larry, what the fuck are you doing here? I thought I told you never to come back— is that my dress?"

MORAL: CHECK THAT YOU HAVE ALL OF THE QUESTIONS BEFORE YOU'RE CONTENT WITH ALL OF YOUR ANSWERS.

"NO REGRETS. I MEAN, **OTHER** THAN THE **DRINKING.** AND THE **FIGHT.** AND THE **POLICE. SEVERAL** REGRETS. **"**

"I didn't *vomit* . . . I just, uh. Well, yeah, I guess that's vomiting, isn't it?"

BROWN-CRESTED POSSEFLOCK

Bulbo localbandus

COMMON NAME
The Horde

HABITAT
Dives, anywhere with bad music on weekdays, and friends of friends' dens.

DIET
Wells, tallboys, and whatever these drink tokens will get you.

CALL
"Yo, we gotta bounce. We, uh, made up the couch. Sorta."

Though never seen individually and by all accounts a social animal, the Posseflock is notoriously bad at group behavior and unable to work together to accomplish even the simplest of tasks. Despite this, however, they are remarkably adept at demolishing a living room. Quite common in densely populated urban areas, the Posseflock cycles from younger brothers' girlfriends' couches to dimly lit beer halls, usually pausing only long enough to screech out distorted mating calls and plow his way through well whiskey. The demands of their flocking instinct usually mean they won't stick around too long in the morning, which is nice for your reserves of cereal, but not so great if you weren't planning on hunting for missing cushions for the next couple hours.

PROS
Might be able to get you on the list.

CONS
Definitely fucked up your toilet.

OWL RESEARCH

ORWELL INSTINCTIVELY STEPPED INTO THE STREET, NOT YET AWARE ENOUGH OF HIS SURROUNDINGS TO BE AWARE OF HOW NOT AWARE HE WAS.

There was a start of movement, and then that ceased, so Orwell dutifully stepped out, obliging this shift in cosmic forces. Suddenly it was cold. Colder than Orwell would have liked.

Orwell realized far too slowly that he had made a terrible mistake.

Orwell's bruised and bloodied brain did its level best to scramble about the information made immediately available to him. He had been on a bus. He was on a bus no longer. He was wherever it was that buses go when they are not needed. Which was where? A bus graveyard?

The notion seemed fanciful, but not in a way that was pleasant or comforting. More like a sinister white van. Regardless of what exactly he was supposed to call it, the one thing that was made immediately clear to Orwell was that he did not want to be here.

This was Suck. This was Cold. This was the kind of place where Funny Stories Come from Later, which was the absolutely last place Orwell wanted to be right now.

The lights of the bus that had brought him
here shut off behind him, and Orwell regretted
everything that he had ever done, or would ever
do, if that was even possible. In this moment
of dulled half clarity, he saw his life for what
it was: a succession of things to feel bad about,
a series of painful punch lines, ending here,
in some darkened bus station.

That was what they were called. Bus *stations*!

More parts of Orwell's operating system came
online, and the situation unraveled. Despite his
self-inflicted head wounds, he had managed
to make it on the right transit route . . . but he
apparently had slept through his stop.

Orwell nodded, a quarter placated. Surely he
couldn't hold himself responsible for falling
asleep! Sleep was a force of nature that simply
couldn't be helped. It was like snowfall, or
bladder control problems.

Returning to the issues at hand, Orwell noted
that though he had established that this was
Not His Problem, it was still, in a very big way,
His Problem. It was just like life to be a dick
about these things.

Orwell waited a moment until he was certain
that he could recognize numbers again and then
checked his watch. Three hours till the service
started up again. What money Orwell had to
his name was currently inside of him, in liquid

form. He was probably going to have to take care of that fairly soon. Orwell sighed. He *could* walk, but that much agency seemed almost an admission of guilt.

And for once, Orwell wasn't guilty.

Orwell curled up on a nearby bench and closed his eyes. There was a lesson in this— somewhere.

MORAL: YEAH, DON'T FALL ASLEEP ON BUSES. JACKASS.

"Dude, calm the fuck down. We got *most* of the vomit."

"Unless it's fried, roasted, or scrambled, it's not going anywhere near my mouth right now."

"Could you just . . . put my laptop . . . like . . . flailing distance from here? Cool."

"I caught up on my sleep, which is good. I did my catching up in a stairwell, which is less good."

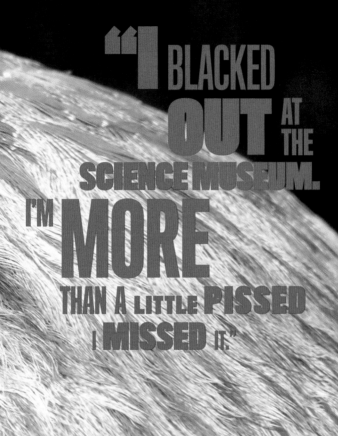

"I BLACKED OUT AT THE SCIENCE MUSEUM. I'M MORE THAN A LITTLE PISSED I MISSED IT."

TAWNY OWL AWOKE THAT MIDAFTERNOON WITH THE DISTINCT IMPRESSION THAT SOMEBODY WAS STEPPING ON HIS BRAIN—AND HAD BEEN FOR SOME TIME.

If you had looked up "degradation" in the dictionary, Tawny wouldn't have been able to read it. He felt that fucking bad. If you could imagine getting a blood transfusion from a truck stop toilet bowl, then you would have an idea of how Tawny felt.

"Holy *shit*," Tawny *would* have said, had not the slightest bit of beak movement jarred loose a pocket of rum. Tawny clenched his entire body against the ensuing wave of nausea. It was unlikely that today was going to be pleasant.

Fractured memories of yesterday put themselves together inside Tawny's head. If there was anything worse than lying here, feeling what it was like to be embalmed alive, it was doing so while remembering what he had done. A pirate costume may have been involved, it wasn't clear.

"At least there wasn't a male prostitute this time," Tawny reasoned.

"Oh *fuck*," he muttered, recalling a bit more of the evening.

Turning his head an ever-so-slight 180 degrees, Tawny eyed a tell-tale black trash can. Things must have *really* gotten bad last night, or else they never would have brought in the big gun. The receptacle of last resort. The trough of shame.

How many evenings had Tawny laughed at lesser fowl while he tossed back boiler-makers as the younger flock lay prostrate at that plastic altar? He, Tawny, who had once chugged a bottle of Midori on a dare and held his composure (hadn't really been able to go near jolly ranchers ever since, but still). Could he really have been brought so low?

Surely not. Tawny was an Owl of Substance. And unless that substance had included Ever-clear, there was no way he had puked last night.

With every last ounce of strength not yet sapped by mai tais, Tawny reached his trembling wing tip over the lip of the unforgiving obsidian and tilted it just enough so he could look inside.

Empty. Yes, he had been brought low, but not that low. It'll take more than a handle of Popov and an escort service to get the better of—

Suddenly Tawny realized that he was very wet. And very indoors. He looked down at his bedding and gave a coconut-flavored sigh.

MORAL:
ALCOHOL.
ALWAYS.
WINS.

OWL WISDOM

1 | If you have to ask if it mixes, it probably doesn't.

2 | The shortest distance between two points is blacking out.

3 | A shot after midnight is a land mine in the morning.

4 If they say it makes you feel better in the morning, and it's not vomiting, they're lying.

5 Bread is your friend. Bread is your *best* friend.

6 Drinking red wine to get drunk is like smoking cigarettes to get a light source. It works, but at what cost?

7 You know what's cheap? Well drinks. You know what's not? Sheets.

8 Red Bull and vodka is a great way to answer any questions you might have about religion.

9 If it's bigger than your head, don't drink out of it.

10 Puke away, not down. There's just more of you down.

11 If you're resting your head on anything that is not a pillow or a body part, you've had too much.

12 If someone says they don't vomit when they drink, be careful. They may actually believe this.

13 If it's a primary color, don't drink it.

"ALRIGHT, ALRIGHT. I'LL ADMIT IT. A PIECE OF PIZZA WOULD HAVE BEEN A GOOD IDEA."

MO' OWL WISDOM

14 | Drunken impulse to eat: Good. Drunken impulse to smoke: Bad.

15 | Drink the opposite color you want to pee.

16 | That cab driver is just being polite. Do him a favor and shut the fuck up.

17 | If it's more than ten bucks, you'd better be buying it for somebody else.

18 | If your drink tastes like candy, you're gonna meet strangers.

19 | See how some shot glasses are the size of fists? Yeah, there's a reason for that.

20 | Fool me once, shame on you. Fool me twice, shame on me. Fool me when I'm drinking, I will probably fight you.

21 | No shit that was a bad idea. You knew that last night, and you were drunk.

22 | It's a lot easier to talk your way out of things when you *don't* have malt-liquor bottles duct taped to your hands.

23 Fruit juice was invented to make it easier to drink poison.

24 Saying you were hit by a car is a lot easier than explaining how you fell *up* the stairs.

25 Drinking contests are pathetic, sophomoric, and a detriment to good booze. Unless you're pretty sure you can take the guy.

26 Beware: The more you drink, the more reasonable a nine-dollar beer will seem.

27 No conversation has ever begun at a dive bar urinal that ended anywhere good. Unzip it, zip it, and get the hell out.

28 Shoveling singles into the jukebox is a great way to tell bartenders that you'd rather listen to Third Eye Blind than reward them for prompt service.

29 When you start getting buzzed, remember this helpful guide: *Belgian* is slang for expensive, *cask conditions* means warm, and *house brew* means runoff from the Budweiser tap.

"In retrospect, a few pieces of pita did not a dinner make."

"I gotta stop yelling at people in Russian when I get wasted. I don't even know Russian!"

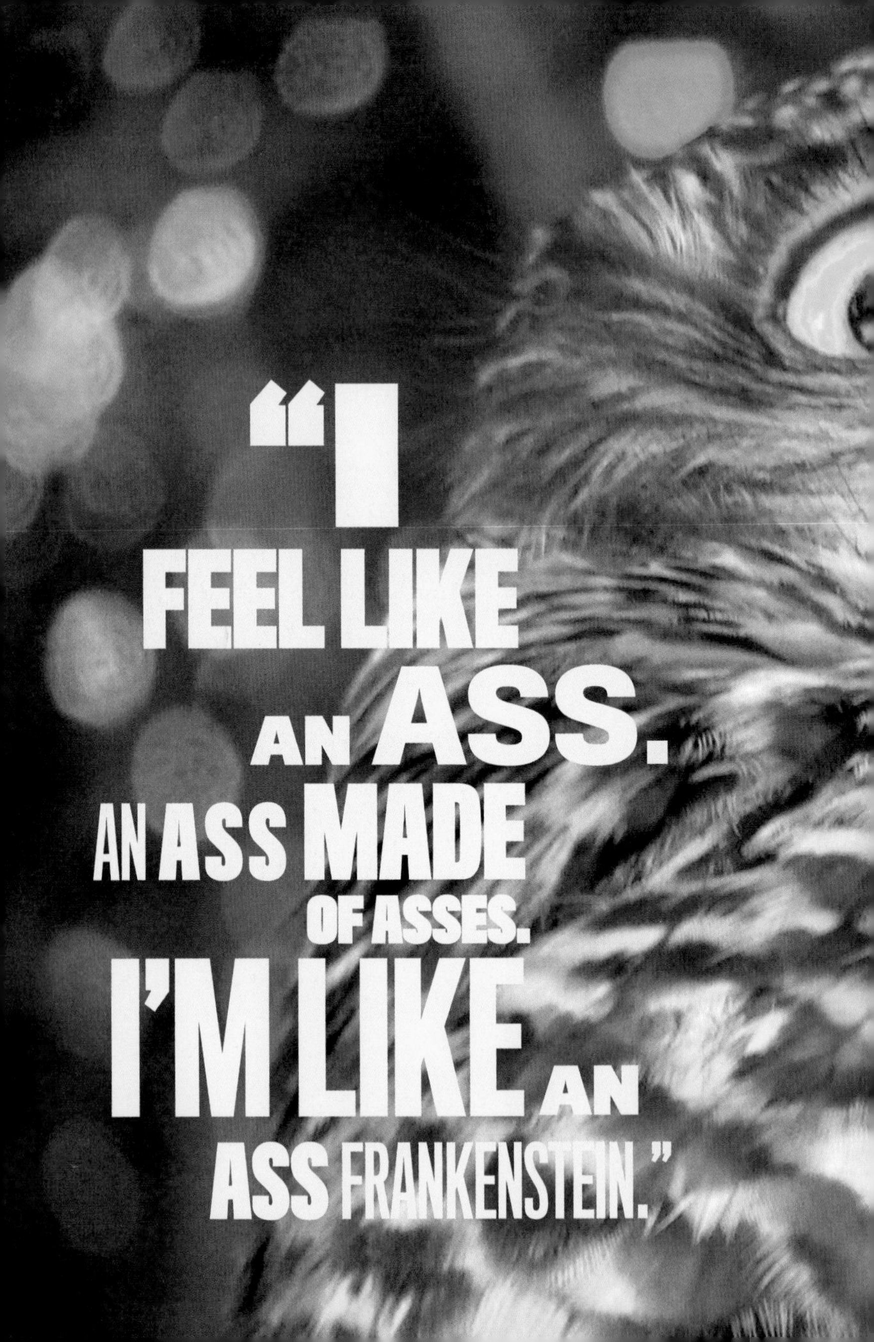
"I FEEL LIKE AN ASS. AN ASS MADE OF ASSES. I'M LIKE AN ASS FRANKENSTEIN."

RED-FLARED CHEAPSKATE

Bubo boozemiser

COMMON NAME
The PBR Roulette

HABITAT
This place he knows with dollar drink specials or wherever you're paying.

DIET
One-dollar drink specials or the cheapest possible round.

CALL
"Oh come on, you get just as drunk!"

OWL RESEARCH

The scourge of mixed flocks, the Cheapskate bides his time on the rounds of others, waiting for the very last possible moment to strike. When decency dictates that he must contribute a pitcher or a shot, he inevitably steps forward with the worst possible thing in stock, transmuting your pint of local microbrew into a Solo cup of urine-flavored fizzy water. Even though he might have put back three Maker's Manhattans on your tab, you'd best believe that reckoning will come in the form of Old Grand-Dad and a defensive shrug. More than simply opting for the wallet-friendly option, the Cheapskate will maintain the objective superiority of *his* selections of down-home, salt-of-the-earth tipples over that highfalutin plutocratic swill of you wine-snob Rockefellers . . . so long as it's his dime. Make the next one a Hendrick's, wouldya?

PROS
Happy with pretty much anything.

CONS
Angry that you're not happy with pretty much anything.

SWELLED RUMPUNCHER

Styrixus whoyoulookingat

COMMON NAME
The Oh Man, He Heard You.

HABITAT
Wherever he hasn't been eighty-sixed yet or places you'd best avoid.

DIET
Boilermakers, shots, or something that little prick just spilled.

CALL
"Why don't you come over here and say that to my face?"

The Rumpuncher *will* fight you. That said, he'll fight *for* you too—he's really not that particular. Come sunrise, so long as he's gone at least a round with *anything*, he'll sleep soundly, calluses dotting his knuckles like morning dew. Drinking is really more of a means to an end for this species—an excuse to go out, meet strange people, and then sock them in their smug fucking faces. As such, the Rumpuncher drinks to get drunk and stay there, downing shots of tequila as if it were some sort of magical hate fuel. Despite the obvious dangers inherent to knocking back a few com-bined with the avian equivalent of a testosterone land mine, most flocks will take care to venture out with at least one Rumpuncher amongst them, if only to cancel out any Rumpunchers encountered in the wild. Loyalty as a justification for kicking someone in the neck is, at the end of the day, still loyalty.

PROS
Great to have on your side.

CONS
Getting punched in the side.

"THIS GUY IS A FUCKING ASS."

"I'm sure I'll be fine in a couple of hours. A couple of hours *after* you've fucked off and left me to my History Channel."

"Tequila me? That's the *worst* me!"

OWL MIXOLOGY

"THE COMING OF AGE"

1 bottle of Boone's Farm
1 empty parking lot
1 album you'll hate later

"THE GRAPEFRUIT OF HATE"

2 bottles of wine
That came out of me?

"THE LAZY PUNCH"

Rum
Pineapple juice?
Fuck it, some Sprite
Rum

"THE NEVER BEEN SICKER"

Beer
Liquor
Oh shit, how did that rhyme go?
Blargh

"THE IMPRESSIN' THE DATE"

1 fancy cocktail bar
6 fancy cocktails
1 week of sandwiches

"THE DUCK DUCK GOOSE"

1 pitcher Hefeweizen
1 pitcher India Pale Ale
1 pitcher Schlitz
Fuck you guys, Schlitz is great!

"Blanket. Blanket closer. Bring."

"The parts of me that have bruises are the parts of me that I shouldn't have been using. I am alarmed."

"This is somebody's fault. Somebody other than me."

"I passed out on my desk. That's like the Internet equivalent of falling asleep on a park bench."

"I'm kinda rethinking my opinions on euthanasia. Just sayin'."

"I'm being punished for something I did in a past life. Apparently, I must have been a real asshole."

"I won't really know the damage until I take a leak. I have my fingers crossed for 'not pissing black.' "

"Fuck. Fucking fuck for shits. Goddamn."

"I'VE FELT BETTER, BUT HEY, I'LL PROBABLY FEEL WORSE. LIKE WHEN I'M DYING. DYING FROM SOMETHING THAT MAKES ME HURT ALL OVER."

WIDE-EYED SNIFFLESNOB

Xenoglaux champagnetastus

COMMON NAME
The Particular Novice

HABITAT
Midscale joints, hotel bars, and not your place, hopefully.

DIET
Don't even get us started.

CALL
"Yikes. You wouldn't happen to have any Macallan ten-year-old around, would you?"

Of all species, the Snifflesnob is one of the last to take flight (and flights), and attempts to compensate for this late start through a poorly studied imitation of the discretion of others. Confusing being obstinate with having experience, the Snifflesnob storms blindly through the minefields of personal taste, pooh-poohing any martini with less than three olives, retching at the sight of golden rum, and refusing to be in so much as the same room with any scotch that is younger than he is. The Snifflesnob can be seen at social gatherings, screwing up his face at the pony keg as if it were an abusive uncle with whom he shares a strained, if outwardly cordial, relationship. Flocking with the Snifflesnob can be a mixed blessing—out in his element, amidst the not-quite-as-nice-as-he-thinks establishments that prey on those with thick wallets and thin palates, the Snifflesnob can be a blast, demanding increasingly expensive (and therefore superior) tipples for his flight mates. Inviting a Snifflesnob to your home, however, is a great way to lose a good bottle, as the Snifflesnob's inherently ignorant generosity will lead him to believe there's nothing at all wrong with uncorking that port your grandfather picked up during World War II.

PROS
Can be trusted for one hell of a round.

CONS
The reason liquor cabinets have locks.

SPECTACLED MOPEFIEND

Pulsatrix weepmongeri

COMMON NAME
The Unpleasant Philosopher

HABITAT
Would Bukowski be here?

DIET
Would Hemingway drink it?
Or, more important, you payin'?

CALL
"Another round, and another round, and another round creeps the petty pace . . . *something*. Shit."

The Mopefiend thinks too much. It drinks too much too, but that really wouldn't be an issue if its drinking would make a damn dent in its thinking, which it doesn't. For the Mopefiend, a jaunt to a liver-destroying dive is more than simply something to do on a Tuesday . . . it is a sacred rite, a chance to commune with high-proofed heavy thinkers who peel back the thin lipids of reality, allowing a glimpse of the endless torment underneath. Darts? Sure, but only until the whiskey-birthed nihilism kicks in. The Mopefiend will tipple, toss back, and carouse with the best of them until some internal quota for self-inflicted misery kicks in, rendering him a sullen, napkin-scribbling shibboleth. In extreme cases, the Mopefiend will produce a journal. Any and all hope from this point on is lost.

PROS
Will do things to a cocktail napkin you wouldn't believe.

CONS
Ignores direct commands to shut the fuck up.

OWL RESEARCH

"It can only get better. Nowhere to go but up. I am *owning* this."

"I won a bet but lost my keys. I think I'm about even."

"What sort of shitty country is this where a guy can't take a quick nap in a parking lot without people being all nosy dicks about it."

"Stop. Stop everything. Everything needs to chill the fuck out."

EVEN MO' OWL WISDOM

30 | I don't care what the song says. Nobody has ever taken a shot and been better for it.

31 | Taking a shot is like leveling a rifle at your future.

32 | *A wine bar?* What, are you celebrating taking the silver at the Ascot Olympics, fancy pants?

33 Why not just throw out all of your antihistamines and give someone thirty dollars to punch you in the face. Same thing.

34 If you can order a salad, then it's not really a bar.

35 If the drink name rhymes, you're not making it home tonight.

36 If I had a dollar for every time I forgot to tip, there would be a hell of a lot fewer bartenders pissed at me.

37 Try to think of regret as a luxury. You gotta draw breath to regret, right? Still a tough sell when you shat on your roommate's futon.

38 "What were you thinking?" is really giving you too much credit. "What were you doing by pure muscle memory?" is far more accurate.

39 Aw, man. *Never* pair sushi with a hard night of drinking. Seriously. You think wasabi hurts going *down*?

40 Yelling out "I love this song!" is the quickest way to inform a room full of people that your higher functions are currently on standby.

41 The later it gets, the more likely it is that you will literally do anything to win a five-dollar bet.

42 | A year and a half of remedial Spanish does not translate into seamless native fluency, no matter how many Dos Equis you downed.

43 | Yes, it is possible to counter-act the hangover with coffee. However, the amount you need will always be one cup more than you've had.

44 | Decaf? *Decaf*? Get the *fuck* out of here! *Pfft*. Decaf.

45 | If you're on the fence about hopping over into full bender territory, ask yourself: Am I going to be having eggs anyway? Why let those embryos go to waste?

OLIVER COULDN'T UNDERSTAND WHY NOBODY WAS DANCING.

"WHY ISN'T ANYBODY DANCING?"

There are other, perhaps more pertinent, questions that one could ask oneself immediately upon being jolted back to understanding, but Oliver had been so keen on losing himself in the first place that he never even noticed when he had left. There was dancing, and then there was dancing alone. Whatever had happened between those two events went unnoticed.

Now, Oliver was still drunk, and always something of an idiot, but there are some things that even a fifth of rum and a handle of stupid can't compensate for. Like the complete absence of any form of music when you are theoretically dancing with a large group of people.

Oliver brought himself as close to a halt that his booze-infused rhythm would allow, which was a much more involved process than you would first expect. Arms akimbo, fists balled, looking to the world like a Rock'em Sock'em Robot that had suddenly lost its nerve, Oliver pivoted from his left to his right and listened.

Nothing. No chunky, funky, bass-heavy groove, no poppy, hoppy, techno-tinged club mix . . . not even one of those god-awful power ballads from that "Begrudgingly Included Eighties Playlist" that had been tossed together in an act of what

Oliver considered outright appeasement. Hell, Oliver would have even been willing to put up with nu metal if it meant anything other than this deafening dead-aired silence.

Oliver thought for a moment and took that last bit back. Yes, by all appearances he was dancing by himself in a darkened, silent basement, but that doesn't mean he had forfeited his dignity.

Oliver thought for a moment and took that last bit back. Okay, so he clearly *had* forfeited his dignity, but at least not quite to the degree that he was going to willingly sit through "Freak on a Leash."

A bit of feedback rang through on the speakers, and Oliver felt a momentary surge of hope that barely lasted long enough for him to grasp. Against all better judgment, he tilted his wrist to the side so he could read the time. Yikes. Well, there you go. Everyone must be asleep.

Oliver vacillated. Both literally and emotionally, maintaining his lonesome march to nowhere, in lockstep with some internalized rhythm, while not sure whether to feel elated or profoundly depressed.

He was the last man movin', *he* had out-grooved all his peers, and lo, it was his booty that still shook when so many others had been flopped onto futons in defeat. He had out-danced music itself, and now, as a reward, he was alone. There was nobody else. He had broken through to the other side and found it to be very lonely.

Oliver slowed. A headache loomed. Regrets began to make themselves known. Muscles that had loyally swayed for him began to revolt. It was late.

Oliver thought for a moment and took that last bit back. It was early.

"Hey, people gotta wake up sooner or later, right?"

Oliver jumped back into it, wondering if there was still an emergency stash of Sparks in the DJ booth.

MORAL: IT ONLY HURTS WHEN YOU STOP.

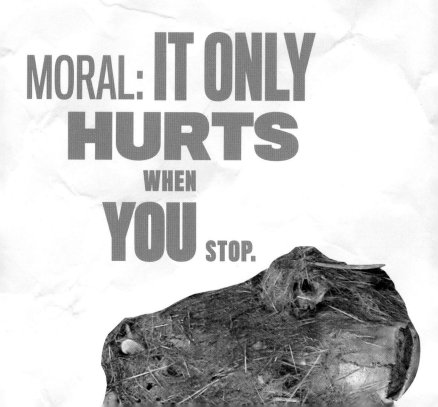

"GETTING A BOTTLE OF WINE WAS LESS EXPENSIVE, BUT ULTIMATELY IT COST SO MUCH MORE."

SHORTLY AFTER YELLING AT HIS SANDWICH, SCOTT CONCLUDED THAT HE WAS NOT DOING SO HOT.

This wasn't quite as smooth a process as one might imagine. Scott made a pretty damn decent case for why the sandwich fucking deserved it. That sandwich was, as Scott pointed out, being kind of a dick.

"Olives. You *hate* olives."

Scott did hate olives. It wasn't fair for the sandwich to go and do that, be full of olives, when it knew—

Scott stopped himself. He was talking about two pieces of pumpernickel here. They knew as much as two pieces of pumpernickel *could* know. That sandwich possessed no more ill will toward him than any other member of the grain family.

"Oh really? Just like that rye bagel you almost choked on last week?"

Scott took a deep breath and sighed heavily, causing a fresh wave of nausea to wash over him. This deflection of personal responsibility schtick had unfortunately become kind of a thing since he started drinking in earnest. The Scott that was, for the most part, a rational being capable of accepting accountability for his actions, was just discovering a whole 'nother part of himself that was liable to blame his misfortune on the machinations of others.

Including, say, the odd inanimate object or two.

Though what it had all boiled down to was Scott's decision to pound one last boilermaker before bedtime (well, trying-to-get-into-bed-time—that thing was a complete asshole last night). Scott found that it was becoming increasingly difficult to fight this instinctual urge of his to weasel out of these so-called statements of fact. What on the surface was a fairly obvious causal relationship between having one too many and feeling a tad bit off became, with the advent of the weasel gene, an elaborate web of misfortunate circumstance and mendacious conspiracy.

Somewhere in the shadows, a sinister figure wrung his hands, cackling triumphantly as Scott decided on a second cup of coffee.

He was being ridiculous, and he was at least aware of it. Last night's soup not pulling its weight in the alcohol absorption department wasn't really the fault of the soup itself. Soup didn't possess any particular responsibility to change its entire consistency when suddenly confronted with a fist-sized deposit of rotgut.

"That is just like you. Defending soup like that."

Scott took a deeper breath and sighed heavily, dislodging a deposit of olives.

"See? Fucking olives! What did I say about the olives! Got it out for you, I swear!"

But what bothered Scott was not that he perceived himself acting like a prat, but that he found it so damn appealing. Soup couldn't *really* shoulder the blame for making the inside of his head feel like a whiskey-soaked dashboard, especially since it lacked anything remotely analogous to shoulders. Scott knew that.

But he sure as hell didn't feel it.

What he *felt* was that he had been betrayed by some fancy-schmancy can of minestrone garbage that was too good to uphold its sacred duty to keep the really nasty stuff from reaching his brain. What he *felt* was that his friends should have pointed out that he should consider slowing down (which they did, several times, but it doesn't really count as an effort on their part unless it succeeds). What he *felt* was that he hadn't gotten a proper amount of sleep the night before (not his fault), drank in the wrong order (beer before liquor, also not his fault), and didn't get enough water (because that bartender was an asshole).

He felt like it wasn't his fault. The fact that he knew it to be was quickly becoming irrelevant.

Scott took his deepest breath and sighed his heaviest sigh. The taste of olives permeated throughout.

He knew it wasn't the sandwich's fault. Whichever one of his roommates had made the thing probably even wanted it to have olives in it, the bastard.

But. But but but.

"But this fucking thing doesn't have to be such a dick about it."

Amen.

MORAL: GO WITH YOUR GUT. THAT'S WHERE YOU PUT ALL THE BOOZE.

OK MO' OWL WISDOM

46 | When your host said, "Knock yourself out," he wasn't really expecting you to take him literally. So he's allowed to be a little pissed.

47 | Not to mention that thing with the wife. Yikes.

48 | After you turn twenty-one, you get exactly one bottle of MD 20/20 per year for high school parking lot nostalgia value. Anything more than that, and you've got a problem.

49 | *I've* got a drinking problem— two wings and only one beak! Hah! Seriously though, this isn't fun anymore, and I think I need some serious help.

50 | The only reason that you should be drinking out of something that wasn't specifically designed for that is so you can win a prize. And that prize better be a hell of a lot more than five dollars.

51 You're gonna lose a few Sundays. You're just going to have to accept that.

52 You know why they call it a well drink? Think "dark, moist, and miserable."

53 If people stop asking you where the scrapes and bruises come from, then you're about due for some serious self-reflection.

54 Dress for success. So long as you define success as "rooting around the bathroom floor for a dropped quarter."

55 | There will always be a few chunks of carrot in there. Nobody knows why.

56 | Drinks in the double-digit range and "I'm fine" are two things that do not belong in the same sentence unless you want to tack on "or so I thought."

57 | Chipped teeth are the upper limit of injuries that are allowed to be met with unsympathetic laughter. Broken bones, sympathetic laughter. The hospital, nervous laughter.

58 Beware of any bar with darts. Clearly your general well-being did not make it onto their list of priorities.

59 Vague memories of dancing on the bar are last night's equivalent of a popped freshness seal.

60 Whatever may be in there, it's nothing good.

61 The more elaborate the tropical name, the more likely it's just a bowl of rum with some pineapple juice floating on top.

"FIRST THINGS FIRST. I'M GONNA LIE HERE FOR A COUPLE HOURS. THEN EVERYTHING ELSE."

MARCUS DIDN'T WAKE UP WITH THAT FAMILIAR CONFUSION OVER WHERE HE HAD MANAGED TO MISLAY HIS PANTS LAST NIGHT.

Instead, he woke up to the far more illuminating question of why he had ever bothered to wear pants in the first place. The entire concept of squeezing himself into two little denim tubes so he could cavort around like some sort of cotton centaur only to inevitably lose them once again. . . . It all seemed somewhat ridiculous in retrospect, really.

"Oh my," Marcus intoned quietly. "I appear to have drunk myself to *enlightenment*."

Despite the constant throbbing, everything appeared, for the first time, truly clear. Even the blurry things. *Especially* the blurry things. From this point on, Marcus would no longer be bound by the petty constraints of his short-sighted fellows, those who saw a sink as only a sink and nothing more. For could it not be said that every sink is, in its own way, also a bucket? And those buckets, are they not toilets as well?

Marcus flushed the sink and could not believe he had ever been so blind. Party mix? Nay. *Breakfast* mix. Half eaten? Sheer prudery. Consider it half *uneaten*. Leftover can of soda? More like . . . oh, oops, that . . . that was a backwash can. Hoo boy. Alright. Marcus was going to have to be a little bit more cautious in these demonstrations. Fortunately, there was a punch bucket nearby, so no harm done.

Marcus chuckled, wiped off a bit of vomit that had been jarred loose, and then chuckled some more. To think that this whole time he had been living in a world full of buckets, and he hadn't even noticed. How could he have been so *blind*? How many needless trips to bathroom stalls, laundry rooms, and alleyways could he have saved?

Marcus lit up a perfectly good cigarette that some fool, clinging to their ignorance, had dropped and then stomped into the ground. If only they knew what they were so casually tossing aside. There were, like, at least a couple of good puffs left on this thing. Marcus would not be above poaching the childish missteps of his lessers. Well, *obviously*, he would be above them in an abstract sense, but that wouldn't stop him from making this into a valuable teaching experience. For was it not said . . . something . . . about something? Somewhere? By somebody?

Marcus was going to enlighten himself up some coffee, and then the specifics of that bit of wisdom would come back to him. As he turned the corner, however, he happened to meet up with his flock, none of whom seemed particularly concerned with unlocking the secrets of the universe. They were more interested in just why the upstairs bathroom smelled like a homeless shelter that catered to the incontinent.

"Marcus! You shit! What the fuck did you do to the sink? And where the hell are your pants?"

Marcus considered his words very carefully. This moment—the first Sermon of Marcus— was to be a momentous occasion, to be remembered years from now as the pivotal point when they allowed themselves to abandon the constraints of—

"DID YOU FUCKING PUKE IN THE PUNCH? *GOD DAMMIT.*"

You know, this was going to be a slightly tougher sell than Marcus had really bargained for.

MORAL:
SPEAK THE TRUTH SLOWLY.

"Hate's not quite what I'm going for. More like dead-brain strangle-lust."

"It's like cross-training. You gotta break your brain down so . . . you know . . .
think. Better. This really isn't helping my argument."

"This too shall pass. And, man, is that turning out to be a bitch."

"I'm pretty sure I lost most of sixth grade last night, but hey, when the fuck am I gonna need to know *algebra*?"

CRIMSON-TINTED MURDERWING

Otus runforyourlives

COMMON NAME
The Hidden Sociopath

HABITAT
He walks among you.

DIET
Fear.

CALL
"Hey, did you know this shit was flammable?"

Unlike its slightly more benign cousin, the Rumpuncher, the Murderwing is outwardly the very model of an almost Zen-like calm. Drink after drink after drink could be hurled against its friendly, unflinching grin, and this would produce almost no discernible change in mood. He'll cover rounds, chuckle at the horrible accusations made against his mother, and even shrug off an errant shoulder and a spilled drink with a smile. There is something soothing and vaguely avuncular about the Murderwing that lures most flock mates into a buzzed sense of serenity. Which only makes it so much more jarring when he sets your tie on fire, or starts hurling bottles of mescal at the DJ. Simply put,

Murderwings are crazy, but not in a way that implies they're self-consciously entertaining or even the source of a good rant about the moon landing. Crazy as in "gleefully amoral." Drinking doesn't bring about any new voices in the Murderwing's head—he won't be writing his name with ketchup packets anytime soon. Nope, booze just drowns out the voice that tells him not to do Very Bad Things. Be afraid.

PROS
Slightly less likely to kill his friends.

CONS
We did say "slightly."

OWL RESEARCH

PRANCING HOPPYCLOP

Asio myjam

COMMON NAME
The Look at Him Go!

HABITAT
Any flat surface with a PA system and booze.

DIET
Whatever mixes with caffeine and sugar.

CALL
"Oh *shit*! This is it!"

You will never love anything the same way that the Hoppyclop loves dancing. Seriously. Offspring, significant others, single-malt scotches, this species will make even your most undying act of fawning devotion come off with the conviction of a diabetic in a candy factory. The Hoppyclop has been modeled, designed, and perfected for the act of flailing about like an idiot. One would think that his frequent bouts of practice would eventually rub off on the guy, but every single last Hoppyclop is invariably a *terrible* dancer . . . if not an extremely entertaining one. So long as the syrupy piston juice of high-fructose cocktails keeps on coming, then Hoppyclop really couldn't care less as he contentedly nuzzles into a world of his own devising. Somewhere between off-tempo techno and early nineties pop punk, somewhere that jerky, arrhythmic lurching and senseless clapping are appreciated, is a place called . . . *home*. Which is less of a saccharin analogy and more of a convenient explanation for why it's a *really* bad idea to fuck with iTunes when Hoppyclops are around. You're never as nasty as when you're defending your domicile.

PROS
Loves this song!

CONS
WHAT THE FUCK! WHO CHANGED IT?

SPECTACLED JAWDROPPER

Pulsatrix mindbloweritti

COMMON NAME
The Enthusiastic Philosopher

HABITAT
Wherever there are minds in darkness. Also big on pub trivia.

DIET
Deep, heady microbrews.

CALL
"But if you look at it like . . . *that*! *Bam*! What did I tell ya?"

Though very closely related to the Mopefiend and liable to share several of its markings (cyan crests, deep ridges, really nice sweaters), the Jawdropper couldn't be more unalike in temperament. It moves forward at a maniacal pace, as if driven forward by some monstrous cerebral engine, knocking back strong drinks and thinking powerful thoughts like it was his job. And honestly, it probably is. The Jawdropper is here to drop some science and sling some lit, living for that moment when his drunken wisdom cracks your thick shell of ignorance, allowing you to douse yourself with some serious grade-A truth. That this has yet to happen to *any* of the people whom he's excitedly, if somewhat incomprehensibly, accosted doesn't bother him in the least. The accosted usually don't mind either. Most of the time he's paying.

PROS
Makes some good points.

CONS
Still won't shut up.

"I was going to ask you to check my pulse. *That's* how bad I feel."

"I'm sorry. I really didn't mean for you to know those things I said.
That . . . that came out wrong."

"**I'LL** JUST ASSUME **THAT** I *HAVEN'T* DONE **IRREPARABLE** DAMAGE TO **MOST** OF **MY** RELATIONSHIPS **UNTIL IT'S** PROVEN OTHERWISE."

OTTO COULDN'T HELP BUT FEEL THAT PERHAPS PEOPLE MIGHT BE OVERACTING, JUST THE SLIGHTEST.

Yes, someone *had* spewed a ring of mulchy brown around the sink in an almost deliberate outline that left the porcelain a mocking alabaster. And yes, Otto *had* been seen wandering around that general vicinity late in the evening, trying desperately to get a grip on that handle he had done a sizable deal of damage to. But those were isolated incidents! Only malicious inference would implicate some untoward connection betwixt the two. Or so Otto maintained.

"You know what they call that in court, my colleagues?" Otto invited his accusers to ponder, pausing a moment not only for effect, but because he was having genuine difficulty remembering.

"Cir . . . *cir* . . . *cumstantial* evidence!" Otto finished with a flourish, inwardly relieved that whatever bundle of neurons that contained the answer had survived last night's impromptu Popov deluge.

For the first time in six years, Otto was grateful for his time spent doing prelaw. Cortices and clusters sprang to life for the first time in half a decade, animating his aching flesh, causing him to resemble a rather poorly puppeteered marionette. Yes, it was certainly true that

Otto had spent a fair bit of the evening irrigating his insides with a generous application of vodka-flavored Windex. Otto could no more deny that than argue that Steve *wasn't* looking more than a little raggedy this morning.

But was it not also accurate that Otto's capacity for intestinal self-control is the stuff of legend, his reputation for regurgitation nigh on spotless, those inevitable missteps minor and contained? Unlike, say, Steve, who once puked *inside* the dishwasher?

Oh, he never mentioned that? Yikes. That would be why we have all those paper plates.

But now is not the time to point fingers or draw conjectures from the long and documented history of Steve's many moments of weakness. Time was ripe for Otto's masterstroke, the hinge of an argument that he had hoped would develop if he just kept talking. Attentions rapt, all eyes on him, Otto drew matters to their now inevitable conclusion.

"What, could any of you offer, was the last foodstuff that I was seen consuming before peacefully passing out to a Netflix stream of old *A-Team* episodes?"

A beat.

"Last week's Chinese?"

"Last week's Chinese. Yes. Thank you. And to the best of your knowledge, does Chinese cuisine contain carrots?"

A second beat.

"Gentlemen, I invite you all to inspect the damage done to our shared domicile, and you will notice the *conclusively* damning presence of said carrots. Carrots that you would not *likely* find in a refrigerated egg roll, but are the crucial component of the Mediterranean dishes enjoyed by one of your number. I will say no more. The rest is up to you."

A third beat. Followed by the laborious, intentioned movement of the would-be mob. Steve didn't stand a chance. That's what the fucker gets for not sharing his lentil soup. Those spring rolls were *terrible*.

Otto returned to his bed and idly picked an orange shred from his beak. *Idiots*.

MORAL: WHAT DO WE KEEP SAYING ABOUT THE CARROTS?

YO MO' OWL WISDOM

62 | It's actually called "punch." What more of a red flag do you need?

63 | The irony value of blacking out on a Mind Eraser is not really worth the jail time.

64 | Compulsive gamblers have it easy. You never go out on a bender and end up with *more money.*

65 Nobody cares about the proper way to prepare absinthe. *Seriously*. Shut the hell up about it.

66 Even though outperforming your colleagues intellectually while extremely hungover can provide a tremendous amount of smug self-satisfaction, it should only be attempted if you really are smarter than everyone else. Otherwise, it's just kinda sad.

67 Did you offer to show anybody your poetry? No? Then you weren't that drunk.

68 Drunk Scrabble: Hilarious. Drunk Jenga: Impossible. Drunk Monopoly: You're going to need some new friends.

69 To avoid getting overwhelmed in the morning, set some reasonable goals. Can you move all of your limbs? You're a winner!

70 Keeping all your vomit in the bucket by your bedside: great. Forgetting about said bucket while trying to get out of bed and ending up ankle-deep in regurgitated guacamole: less great.

71 Yeah, you sure made major headway on that novel last night, champ.

72 Put the acoustic guitar down. Just put it down and walk away.

73 If the combined value of your drinks is greater than or equal to the value of the item you're currently holding, you should put it down immediately.

74 The Internet. You want none of that, trust me.

75 Seriously, any drunk is too drunk to ride them Interwebs.

76 All I did was change my status to "realizn ho much i totalyl in luve with you gus" and I'm still getting shit about it.

77 A pitcher is the smallest unit of friendship.

"LIVER DAMAGE, SCHMIVER SCHMAMAGE. HAND OVER THE FUCKING PILLS."

MO' MO' OWL WISDOM

78 | Franzia. It's liquid that came in a box. That was your first clue. Mother Nature was not invited to that baby shower.

79 | With top-shelf liquor, you're not paying for taste, you're paying for purity. In other words, you're paying *not to go blind.*

80 | Happy Hour, you are the source of so much sadness.

81 | Cheap beer and expensive cigarettes — two things you should get out of your system after college.

82 | Taking a flaming shot is a great way to demonstrate to others that you've managed to survive this long thanks only to the constant intervention of a bemused higher power.

83 | When it comes to proof, aim for the eightieth percentile. Ninety to one hundred is hitchhiking on the highway to the danger zone. Anything above that, and you'll be getting the worst kind of extra credit.

84 If you're drinking wine out of anything other than a wine glass, you're getting fucked up.

85 Homemade sangria is a great way to liven up any gathering. Or you can just set the place on fire. Same thing, really.

"YEAH, THAT WOULD BE **BLOOD.** AND **MY LEFT ARM DOESN'T** *SEEM* TO BE WORKING. **WELL,** THIS IS OFF TO A GREAT START."

HAVING NOT YET OPENED HIS EYES, WESLEY WAS FIRST INCLINED TO BELIEVE THAT HE HAD SUFFERED A MILD STROKE.

His brain wearily barked orders to his left wing, demanding that it move. The wing, taking stock of the brain's injuries, deemed it no threat and continued to slumber peacefully.

Despite all this, Wesley was struck by a strange sense of calm. So his left wing seemed to be paralyzed. No biggie. Fuck that guy. He was a right-wing man all the way.

A feverish wave of ache radiated from his body like an extra blanket. A long day lay ahead of him, full of hour-long craps, pants-less History Channel viewing, and MSG-saturated takeout. As far as being miserable goes, he was content.

His first mistake was opening his eyes. His second mistake was focusing them.

And then there was mistake number three: dallying with clarity.

"Where the fuck did I get a Blink 182 poster? Did I rob my *childhood* last night?"

It was, after all, a fairly reasonable question. But being reasonable was the last thing Wesley needed at this point. Mistake four came riding in on the terrible wings of comprehension.

"I do not own a Blink 182 poster."

No, he did not. But he remembered who did. He also remembered why the DVD menu of *Saved by the Bell* was running in an endless loop. And why he still couldn't move his left wing.

Mistakes five, six, and seven, respectfully.

His right wing was far more accommodating, and he used it to gently massage the feathers of his now-throbbing temples. He would not be spending this day holed up on his beloved futon, food within comfortable flailing distance. Nor would there be Band-Aid beer soothing his damaged brain, or even a reward nap to celebrate that lap around the kitchen counter.

What he *would* be doing, however, is having a long series of uncomfortable discussions and dipping deep, *deep* into his bullshit reserves. And most likely, programming a new phone number in his phone as DO NOT ANSWER.

"Hello there, sexy." A wine-stained chirp came from somewhere beneath his left shoulder.

"H . . . hi, Candice," rejoined a wincing Wesley.

Today was going to *suck*.

MORAL:
UNTIL YOU'RE
IN A **PINE BOX,**
IT'S ALWAYS
TOO EARLY
TO DECLARE VICTORY.

"Ah. *Ahhhhh*. It's my, uh, my sinuses. Yep. Fuckin' sinuses."

"The back entrance is just an easier one to leave from, that's all.
Don't make this into a thing."

"It's the weather. The weather and the humidity. The weather, the humidity, and that quart of vodka."

"Dude, I already told you it was my bad. That about covers it for reasonable expectations right now."

"THE NITPICKING ASSHOLE"

Rum
Coke
Well, it's not a Cuba Libre without
the lime, is it?

"THE AWKWARD SILENCE"

1 Coffee
0 Shots
Gotta make it to my meeting.

"LOOK, WE NEED TO TALK"

2 friends
4 pitchers
1 bed
You've been avoiding me.

"THE ANSWER"

1 bottle of tequila
1 worm
Dash of curiosity
Oh God, I can't vomit enough.

"THE I'VE LIVED A GOOD LIFE"

1 can Red Bull
Vodka
He will be missed.

"THE TAKE OUR WORD FOR IT"

1 bowl of sake
You'll regret that!
1 new experience
Alright dude, we warned you.
1 what the fuck is this shit?
Ha ha, dude, what did we say?

"THE CELEBRATION"

1 ounce good news
Several drinks

"THE COMMISERATION"

1 ounce bad news
Several drinks

"THE MOTHERFUCKER"

1 shot of tequila
Goddamn.

"THE TEARJERKER"

6 drinks
1 recent breakup
Sarah, oh God, why?

"THE I NEVER LIKED YOU"

4 draft beers
1 old friend
1 old grudge
2 shots
Minus 1 old friend

"THE COMA"

1 that guy
1 "Did I hear *birthday*?"
1 hospital

"THE RENT'S A LITTLE SHORT THIS WEEK"

1 paycheck
1 terrible grasp of finance
5 microbrews

"THE WHY AM I AN ASHTRAY?"

Several drinks
1 lapsed habit
No running

"THE THIS TASTES FUNNY"

5 beers
0 tip
1 pissed off bartender

"THE HUBRIS"

1 late lunch
1 heavy snack
No dinner
1 dry heave

"I am here. I am working. I am doing this. This is happening. *Damn it.*"

"All of my clothes are balled up by the door. It looks like I molted.
I molted a sweater."

"I made it halfway onto the bed before I passed out. That's still a win."

"I may have miscalculated how cool I would be with this in the morning."

"MY EYES... MY EYES ARE TRYING TO ESCAPE."

IF YOU HAD PRESSED OTIS TO SUMMARIZE HIS CURRENT SITUATION IN A SINGLE WORD . . . WELL, HE WOULDN'T HAVE BEEN ABLE TO DO SO.

If you had checked back in a couple of hours, when he had begun to regain parts of simple speech, he would have mumbled something that might have sounded like "damp."

Moisture was currently *the* defining force of Otis's life. There was nothing about Otis at the moment that could be understood separately. He was wet, he wasn't terribly happy about being wet, and if he was to have any major goals for the future, they would involve not being wet anymore. Otis had spent the greater part of his last conscious hour bemoaning to anyone who would listen how he felt a crippling lack of direction in his life, giving him no choice but to huddle here under a Ping-Pong table, downing something that was at least partially concocted from cleaning fluid.

Had anybody actually *listened*, they probably would have pointed out the inherent irony that Otis had finally discovered a sense of purpose: finding a towel. Probably. Otis wasn't too terribly popular these days. Not since the mental breakdown right in the middle of a very heated game of beer pong.

Otis shifted, or twitched, or whatever it's called when you poke something with a stick and it isn't quite dead. The uneven amount of misery that ensued led Otis to a rather uncomfortable conclusion. And considering that even a best-case scenario here would still leave Otis sopping wet and shuddering on the floor of a basement rec room, "relatively uncomfortable" was not a direction Otis was interested in heading.

The damp was uneven. Parts of Otis were simply moister than others. This did not bode particularly well for the nature of future discoveries. Bad news is so much better when it's consistent.

Otis ran through a series of scenarios in his aching neural pathways.

Scenario A, filed under more hopeful, less likely: At some point last night, he had gone on an impromptu dive in a nearby body of water, discovered submerged riches, and passed out from sheer elation and excitement. Obviously he had dried off more in some places than others.

Scenario B, filed under less ideal, more likely: He sat underneath a gaming table, drank a bottle of something cheap and terrible, then pissed himself before being spat on in disgust.

Scenario B *did* give a fairly satisfactory explanation for what appeared to be tears. If he had been feeling slightly more pro-

Otis and slightly less absolutely disgusted
with the shame-soaked thing he had become,
it's possible that he could have argued that
those could have been tears of joy, perhaps
celebrating Scenario A's good fortune.

Otis's brain had recovered enough for
him not to defend himself. It sure as shit
wasn't *raining*.

Sunk as low as one could be, lying on the floor,
Otis gave something that was a reasonable
facsimile of a shrug and opened his eyes.

Well, shit. It *was* raining. Otis . . . hadn't really
considered that as a viable option. That's,
uh, that's not so bad. At least he had gotten
most of his head underneath shelter. That
explained . . . well, wait, actually that didn't
explain much. How was it *raining*?

Otis lay there in a state of confused elation
familiar to many a heavy drinker. He was still
being presented with an impossible scenario,
but at least it was one that wasn't his fault.
A few memories popped back into place,
a few more conclusions were drawn.

"Whose fucking idea was it to move the pong
   table to the *roof*?" Otis emphatically muttered
   to anybody who would listen.

"Yours," they would have responded,
   if anybody had.

MORAL:
THERE ARE
WORSE THINGS
IN HEAVEN
AND EARTH,

HORATIO,
THAN ARE DREAMT OF
IN **YOUR** PHILOSOPHY.

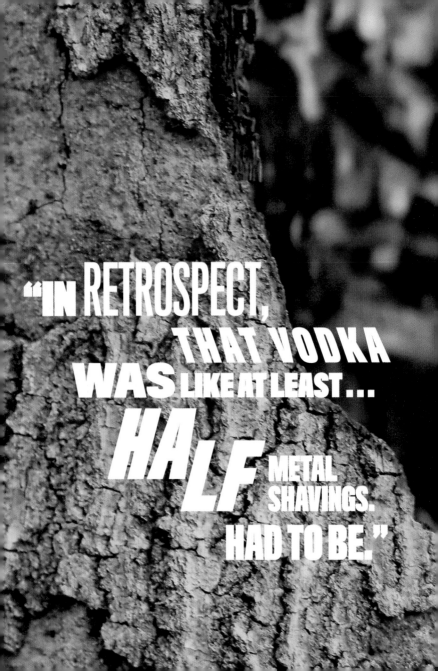

"That ride to the airport? Not really happening. If you can find my pants, you're welcome to grab some cab fare from them."

"Whatever you're dealing with can wait until I'm able to pretend I care."

"That wasn't a bar. That was just some dude's house. And we weren't eighty-sixed, we were almost arrested."

"Well, *gallon jug* just entered and exited my vocabulary in one fell swoop."

"*Heh.* I am not even going to pretend like that went well."

"Go now. Warn others so that they may learn from my mistakes. And pick up some Powerade while you're at it."

"So we're agreed. No hanging out after nine or more drinks."

"I'm updating my list of places I've pissed. A lot more than I'm really
 comfortable with, honestly."

"We cleaned up the living room a bit, but the kitchen was like that when we got here."

"I wrote myself an apology last night. Then about halfway through I just doodled a bunch of dicks."

"WHAT **ARE** THE **CHANCES** THAT **WE** COULD JUST **ADD THIS TO** THE **BLACKOUT?** IS THAT **POSSIBLE?**"

"I'm 95 percent sure that's red wine coming out of my mouth. The alternative's blood, so maybe that's just wishful thinking."

"What part of my vomiting in a bucket wasn't your clue to leave?"

"I'm debating whether to apologize or just get a new group of friends.
There are merits to both."

"You all saw it! I had no choice! He had already paid for the shot!"

"I distinctly remember knocking this over so I'd have to pick it up in the morning. Man, I can be a prick to myself sometimes."

"I spent the last half hour willing myself into the future. So far it seems to be working."

"I remember a lot of laughing, and none of it being my own. That's bad."

"I'm really hoping that the taste in my mouth is just *like* lighter fluid, and not, you know . . . just saying."

"You may or may not be out of bread. I vaguely remember making at least a dozen sandwiches."

"You kept trying to use your car keys to pop open the trunk of your bicycle. At first it was funny, but then we realized you don't actually have car keys."

"Do me a favor and just toss a paper towel roll in this general direction.
I appear to be leaking."

"Shutupshutupshutup. Pleasepleaseplease."

"SO, WE'RE SETTLED—WE'LL SAY WE'RE SORRY, AND THEN WE'LL SEE IF ANYBODY KNOWS WHAT WE'RE TALKING ABOUT."

"I'm getting up. I'm getting up and I'll go places. You're welcome."

"Sun? No. *Denied.*"

"It's like I'm a collage made of *scabs*."

"That twelve-dollar drink hit my fifteen-dollar burger and the next thing you know, I was pukin' out a millionaire's milkshake."

"I can't tell what part of this is the getting kicked in the head and what part is just the general agony. I tipped, right? So, we're absolutely ruling out a deliberate poisoning."

"I'm angry at the *concept* of existing. That's where I am right now."

"**I** SHOWERED **BUT** THE SMELL'S *STILL THERE.* I DON'T REALLY WANT TO THINK ABOUT WHAT THAT MEANS **ABOUT MY** INSIDES."

"Alright . . . I'm taking a crap, and if I don't feel better after that,
then I'm out of ideas."

"To be fair, all the stuff I blacked out was pretty boring. Like brushin'
my teeth and shit."

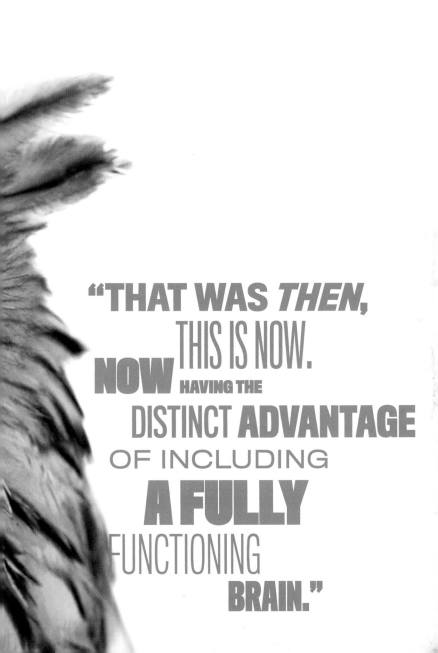

"THAT WAS *THEN*, THIS IS NOW. NOW HAVING THE DISTINCT ADVANTAGE OF INCLUDING A FULLY FUNCTIONING BRAIN."

GLOSSARY

ALCOHOL TERMINOLOGY

BOILERMAKER
We'll put it like this: Nobody drinking a boilermaker has ever been *surprised* that they got arrested.

MARTINI
You know that little bowl of peanuts they have at bars? This is like that, except it's got olives. And it's full of gin.

PUNCH
Actually, that one's pretty self-explanatory.

SHOT
The base unit of shame.

WELL DRINK
That'd be the "scummy hole" kind of well. It's also where you'll probably be waking up the next morning.

SPIRITS

EVERCLEAR

GIN
"The poet's spirit." Translation: It's usually pretty cheap, and nobody wants to steal it.

HENDRICK'S
Proceed with caution: Anybody who can afford to get drunk on Hendrick's is wealthy and dangerous. (See also: *gin*)

MACALLAN
Fuck caution. Anybody who can afford to get drunk on Macallan is a supervillian. (See also: *Scotch*)

MAKER'S MARK
Nice going, Steve. Now the Simmons are gonna start locking the liquor cabinet. (See also: *whiskey*)

MIDORI
Just in case you were wondering what it's like to vomit a rave.

POPOV
Grey Goose in a guest's glass. (See also: *vodka*)

PORT
Nobody under the age of alive drinks port.

RUM (DARK AND LIGHT)
Hey, if you figure out the difference between those two, more power to ya. Every time we think we've finally gotten it, we're already naked in somebody's trunk.

SAKE

Have you ever had a sake hangover? No, exactly. Nobody has. It's impossible to drink that much of it.

SCOTCH

Father-bonding in a bottle. (See also: *whiskey*)

TEQUILA

Less of a spirit, per se, and more of a silent pact to do something felonious.

VODKA

Tastes like nothing going down. Tastes like everything coming up.

WHISKEY

Intended for people who feel deep and moody on the inside, and want to get that violently expelled as quickly as possible.

MIXERS

FRUIT

"Hey, you know what all this nutritious food is missing?" "What?" "Poison!" "Right on!"

PINEAPPLE JUICE

Mix together with rum to create every single tropical drink. Ever.

RED BULL

What? Are you in a rush to do something stupid?

BEER

DOS EQUIS

Don't lie: You bought it for the ad campaign. In all fairness, it was a damn good ad campaign.

DRAFT

"You got this in a bucket?"

HEFEWEIZEN

How do you get away with ordering a fruitier beer? You order it in German.

INDIA PALE ALE

Pay for three. Feel like six. Vomit for nine.

MALT LIQUOR

Place those 40 ounces next to your head. Give that a little think.

MICROBREW
"Man, had a rough day at the alt-weekly."

PBR
"Man, had a rough day at my blog."

TALLBOY
The size of two fists stacked on top of each other. There's reason for that.

WINE

BOONE'S FARM
See: "Your uncle has a headache and needs to borrow a few bucks. Don't tell anybody."

FRANZIA
See: "Your mom's book club has a headache."

MAD DOG 20/20
See: "Who gave your uncle money? Now we need to reupholster the futon."

RED
See: "Mom's got a headache."

SANGRIA
See: "*Tu mamá tengo dolor de cabeza.*"

WHITE
See: "Mom's got a headache and we're having fish tonight."

RECOVERY

COFFEE
Literally the opposite of drinking water. And yet there you are— chugging it. What the hell is wrong with you?

POWERADE
Great as a mixer or for rehydrating in the morning. Sports? No clue.